EATING DISORDERS
Pocketbook

By Pooky Knightsmith

D1584086

Published by:

Teachers' Pocketbooks
Laurel House, Station Approach,
Alresford, Hampshire SO24 9JH, UK
Tel: +44 (0)1962 735573
Fax: +44 (0)1962 733637
Email: sales@teacherspocketbooks.co.uk
Website: www.teacherspocketbooks.co.uk

*Teachers' Pocketbooks is an imprint of
Management Pocketbooks Ltd.*

Series editor: Linda Edge.

© Pooky Knightsmith 2012.

This edition published 2012.

ISBN: 978 1 906610 49 4

E-book ISBN: 978 1 908284 93 8

British Library Cataloguing-in-Publication
Data – A catalogue record for this book is
available from the British Library.

Design, typesetting and graphics by Efex Ltd.
Printed in UK.

Contents

Foreword

I was a complete nightmare for my teachers at school, struggling with an eating disorder and determined to make it as difficult as possible for anybody to help me. I'll always be grateful to my teachers who were caring and supportive, but my eating disorder was contained rather than beaten and my university days saw my weight plummet to five stone. When I was finally recovered, I looked back at the years I'd lost and realised that if only appropriate support and advice had been available to my school, things need never have got so bad. But even then – a decade later – there was little relevant support available to teachers, and so my mission began.

In 2008, as director of training for Creative Education Ltd, I developed a one-day eating disorders course for school staff which flew off the shelves. It led to me being invited to research a PhD on the topic by the Institute of Psychiatry – home to a leading eating disorders unit at the Maudsley Hospital. For the last few years I have worked alongside internationally renowned eating disorders experts Prof Ulrike Schmidt and Prof Janet Treasure, using my education and training background to take their clinical and psychiatric expertise and apply it to a school setting.

Foreword

The most important input to my research has come from the 800 school staff and 500 pupils I've been privileged to work with. These volunteers have shared their experiences, good and bad, made suggestions, recommendations and tested ideas in their schools. You'll notice that this book is filled with quotes – every one comes directly from a conversation I've had with a pupil or teacher.

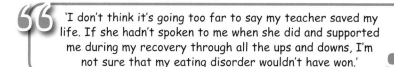

'I don't think it's going too far to say my teacher saved my life. If she hadn't spoken to me when she did and supported me during my recovery through all the ups and downs, I'm not sure that my eating disorder wouldn't have won.'

Statistically speaking, one student in each of your classes is at risk of an eating disorder. This book is designed to give you the information, advice and practical ideas you need to offer your pupils life-changing support.

Foreword

Written primarily, though not exclusively, for school staff, this book is particularly suitable for anyone working in a school setting, including teachers, pastoral staff, teaching assistants, learning support assistants and school counsellors.

The first two thirds of the book are aimed at all staff, and will help you to identify pupils at risk of the three major eating disorders: Anorexia Nervosa (referred to throughout as anorexia), Bulimia Nervosa (referred to throughout as bulimia) and Binge Eating Disorder. You'll also learn how to encourage students to share their concerns and how to handle those first difficult conversations. More in-depth strategies for supporting recovery are covered in the final third of the book – this is useful information for all staff, though the interventions are usually implemented by those with specific pastoral or management responsibilities.

Introduction to Eating Disorders

 Life with an Eating Disorder

 Risk Factors and Warning Signs

 Encouraging Pupils to Share Concerns

 Talking it Through

 Next Steps

 Practical Support

 Keeping on Track

Introduction to Eating Disorders

What is an eating disorder?

First things first – what is an eating disorder?

The thing that all eating disorders have in common is the use of food and weight as a coping mechanism. This can play out in many different ways including over-eating, over-dieting or using methods such as vomiting to remove food from the body.

Young people with eating disorders typically have very low self-esteem and place huge importance on their weight and body shape.

Whilst eating disorders are readily dismissed by some as a teenage fad, the truth is that they are **a serious mental health disorder** affecting up to **5% of school pupils**. These young people need our help and support to overcome their illness. With this support, alongside medical help (see page 17) they have every chance of returning to full health.

Eating disorder mythology debunked

There are lots of commonly held misconceptions about eating disorders. Before we go any further, let's set the record straight on a few things:

Talking about eating disorders will start an epidemic.

FALSE! Eating disorders are complex and won't suddenly occur. Talking about them may raise awareness and help you recognise cases but that's a GOOD thing.

Eating disorders are just a passing phase.

FALSE! Very few eating disorders will be cured without support. The delay in support caused by watching and waiting for them to pass can be very damaging.

It's normal – all teenagers diet.

FALSE! Many teens diet, but eating disorders are not normal. We'll discuss how to spot the difference between a diet and an eating disorder later. (Page 49)

He can't be that ill, his school work is fine.

FALSE! Pupils with eating disorders often have obsessive, perfectionist personalities. It is not unknown for them to forfeit sleep entirely to gain an A grade. This is not healthy.

What is anorexia?

Anorexia is the most high profile of the major eating disorders and the one you are likely to have heard most about. (Shocking images always attract media attention and pictures of people who have severely restricted their food intake fit that bill.) Anorexics will have some or all of these symptoms:

- Underweight
- Trying hard to lose more weight
- Believe they're fat when they're not
- Terrified of gaining weight

- Obsessively count calories
- Periods stop
- Exercise hard to aid weight loss
- Completely controlled by the disease

Diagnostic criteria* for anorexia include intense fear of gaining weight, a refusal to maintain body weight above 85% of the expected weight for a given age and height, and – for females – three consecutive missed periods. In addition, there will be either refusal to admit the seriousness of the weight loss, an undue influence of shape or weight on self-image, or a disturbance in how one's shape or weight is experienced.

*Diagnostic and Statistical Manual of Mental Disorders. 4th Edition.(DSM-IV). (2000)

Understanding anorexia

'I first started losing weight because I liked the feeling of control it gave me, but now I can understand that the anorexia was actually controlling me.

The anorexic voice inside my head wouldn't let me eat, or even drink, some days and it made me stay awake at night, exercising to lose more weight.

Everyone said I was fading away but the thinner I got, the fatter I felt. I would look in the mirror and cry as I saw this ugly whale looking back at me.

I always had a target weight, and every time I made it I'd realise I was still fat so I'd aim for a new, lower target.'

Around 5% of cases of anorexia are fatal.
(Clinical Knowledge Summaries Service)

What is bulimia?

Bulimia is characterised by the **binge-purge cycle**. Sufferers eat a large amount of food and then remove this food from their bodies, usually by vomiting or using laxatives.

Many bulimics try hard to diet, but end up bingeing if they slip up on their diet or have to face a difficult situation in their life. This results in feelings of guilt and the need to purge, followed by a promise to diet harder, better and longer next time. The cycle is similar for many sufferers, though the length of time between binges varies from a few hours to several days. Bulimia can go undetected for years as sufferers tend to have a roughly normal weight.

Diagnostic criteria for bulimia*: repetitive episodes of binge eating compensated for by excessive or inappropriate measures to avoid gaining weight. Self-evaluation unduly influenced by shape and weight.

*Diagnostic and Statistical Manual of Mental Disorders. 4th Edition.(DSM-IV). (2000)

Strict dieting → Diet slips or difficult situation arises → Binge eating triggered → Purging to avoid weight gain → Feelings of shame & self-hatred → Strict dieting

Understanding bulimia

'More than anything in the world, I wanted to be anorexic. I tried really hard to starve myself but it would only last a few hours, then the cravings would get too much and instead of eating a normal meal, I'd find myself bingeing.

I ate so much. It was disgusting. I was meant to be saving for my gap year, but I was secretly spending all my money on chocolate bars. I could eat up to twenty at a time. Then of course I'd suddenly realise what I'd done and I'd panic about how to get it all back out.

Often, I spent longer throwing up than eating. Every time I'd promise myself I'd stick to my diet this time, but I just couldn't do it.'

As many as 8% of women experience some bulimic symptoms at some point in their lives. (NHS, 2011)

What is binge eating disorder?

Binge eating disorder, also known as compulsive eating, is an illness typically characterised by a pattern of eating large quantities of – often unhealthy – food over a short period of time. Usually within about two hours. It is the most prevalent eating disorder.

Binge eating can take a few different forms. Many sufferers binge on large volumes of food in short periods, whereas others will eat smaller volumes more frequently – sometimes constantly grazing but never feeling full. What all binge eaters have in common is a lack of control and an inability to stop themselves from eating. Binge eating is often dismissed simply as greed. This is not the case. Binge eating is an eating disorder and sufferers need just as much help and support as bulimics and anorexics. Key characteristics are:

- Being overweight
- Having low self-esteem
- Weight that increases over time
- Lack of control over how much is eaten
- Inability to change, even when health is at risk

Binge eating disorder is currently classed as 'eating disorders not otherwise specified'. Diagnostic criteria are likely to be listed in future editions of DSM (see page 10).

Understanding binge eating disorder

'The thing that hurts most of all is that people think it's entirely my fault. They think that I should just eat less and exercise more. But it's not that easy.

It feels like someone is actually forcing me to eat – even as I'm doing it I'm screaming inside 'No – you'll get even fatter' but my body goes onto auto pilot.

After a while, the food starts to numb my pain so I keep on eating because I feel numb and safe, just for a little while.'

Approximately 2% of adults are thought to be affected by binge eating disorder. (NICE, 2011)

The eating disorder continuum

Appearances can be deceptive. Despite having different impacts on body weight, at their heart the three major eating disorders have a lot in common. Those who suffer from one of these disorders will:

- Have low self-esteem
- Be controlled by food and weight
- Value themselves according to their shape and weight
- Be unable to change without help and support

Treatment

There is a range of treatments available for eating disorders and sufferers may be treated either as inpatients or outpatients. There is often a concurrent focus on reaching a healthy weight (either by gaining weight or losing it) though dealing with the underlying psychological issues is the more important part of treatment.

Treatments include:

- **Cognitive Behavioural Therapy (CBT)** – aims to alter behaviour by changing the way in which the sufferer thinks about food, their weight and their appearance

- **Dietary Counselling** – a talking therapy that works towards maintaining a healthy diet

- **Psychodynamic Therapy** – explores life experiences and their impact on the sufferer's current behaviour

- **Medication** – some sufferers are treated with antidepressants

- **Family Therapy** – the sufferer's family is supported in playing an active, positive role in recovery

Eating disorders don't discriminate

A lot of people think that eating disorders only affect certain types of people. This is especially the case with anorexia, which is commonly considered a teenage girls' disease. It's true that many people with anorexia are white, middle class, high achieving teenage girls. But they don't account for all cases: for instance, **one in ten people with anorexia is male**.

Another commonly held misconception is that certain ethnic groups are not affected by eating disorders. The evidence shows that Asian girls are particularly at risk of bulimia and incidences of eating disorders amongst Afro-Caribbean students are also on the increase.

Absolutely anyone can suffer from an eating disorder – black or white, young or old, boy or girl, able or less able. Statistics from 35 NHS hospitals in England reported in July 2011 showed that in the three preceding years almost 200 children aged between five and nine were hospitalised as the result of an eating disorder.

Eating disorders don't discriminate. It's important to keep your eyes open for cases even where you might not expect to find them. Otherwise you might miss what's right under your nose.

Boys get eating disorders too

'I spent every breaktime and lunchtime training in the gym, or running laps. I didn't have time to eat and I didn't want to. I was so focused on getting fit and besides, even the thought of eating made me feel sick and panicky.

It was only when I passed out at school that people started to realise something was wrong. It took ages for me to get the referral that helped me in the end, though, because no one, not even the doctors, considered that I could be anorexic. After all, I'm a boy. Boys don't get anorexia. Or at least, that's what we all thought.'

How YOU can help

By now, you might be wondering what you can do to help. The answer is, 'Quite a lot' :

'I don't think it's going too far to say my teacher saved my life. If she hadn't spoken to me when she did and supported me during my recovery through all the ups and downs, I'm not sure that my eating disorder wouldn't have won.'

'Our school counsellor was this amazingly approachable person. She was kind but matter of fact. I knew I could trust her and that she'd be able to help. She never once let me down and I always felt like she was on my side and never judging me like other people.'

Some of the things you can do include:

- Keeping an eye on pupils at risk
- Providing a safe place for pupils to talk
- Acting as a bridge between pupils, friends and family
- Offering support during the recovery process
- Looking out for warning signs
- Being supportive and honest

In the rest of this book we'll be looking at practical ideas for supporting pupils with eating disorders. As your knowledge increases so will your confidence in dealing with this subject.

Introduction to Eating Disorders

 Life with an Eating Disorder ◀

 Risk Factors and Warning Signs

 Encouraging Pupils to Share Concerns

 Talking it Through

 Next Steps

 Practical Support

 Keeping on Track

Life with an Eating Disorder

Why do people suffer from eating disorders?

Sufferers give lots of different reasons for their eating disorders – and they're not all about wanting to look like the models in Vogue. Far from it:

CONTROL
'My life felt like a great big mess and food was the only thing I could control.'

PUNISHMENT
'I hated myself for not being perfect at school, for being a bad daughter, for not being popular enough. Starving myself felt like a good punishment.'

SPECIAL
'For the first time in my life, people noticed me. It made me feel special.'

PURE
'I like to feel empty; it makes me feel clean and pure inside. The best kind of empty is when I haven't eaten or drunk anything at all.'

SCARED
'I couldn't have food anywhere near me without having a panic attack; it was horrible. How can you eat when food makes you pass out with fear?'

A mile in their shoes

Life is very difficult for someone with an eating disorder. Over the next few pages we'll see how their lives are made complicated by:

1. A preoccupation with food.
2. 'Thinspiration'.
3. Pro-ana and pro-mia websites.
4. The eating disorder voice.
5. Increasing isolation.

1. A preoccupation with food

Whether they are bingeing on 5,000 calories a day, or restricting themselves to fewer than 200, young people with eating disorders tend to have a crippling preoccupation with food. There are very few times when a sufferer is not thinking about food in some way, shape or form. They might be agonising over what they've eaten, thinking about what and when they're next going to eat, fantasising about their favourite food, or planning how to avoid their next meal.

Their obsession with food makes it very difficult for them to focus on anything else. This is one reason sufferers find it hard to participate in class. It's very difficult to focus on long division when your thoughts are dominated entirely by your next meal.

'My teacher was like, 'Shelly, are you with us?' She'd asked me some question about Macbeth but I couldn't have cared less. I'd bought some Mars Bars at lunchtime and I knew they were right there in my bag and I couldn't think of anything else.'

2. 'Thinspiration'

Eating disorders sufferers are particularly sensitive to the images of the 'perfect body' we are bombarded with every day in adverts, magazines and on TV and the internet.

Whilst eating disorders are not always fuelled by a drive for thinness, most sufferers have huge issues with their weight and shape and think that everyone around them is judging them by their size. Constant reminders of the 'thin ideal' can further fuel eating disordered thoughts.

Many sufferers will collect images of models or skinny celebrities for times when they need to feel inspired to restrict their food intake, or purge themselves of the calories they've eaten. This is very easy on the internet using sites like Pinterest or Tumbler where sufferers can create visual scrapbooks of skinny images, often referred to as 'Thinspiration' or 'Thinspo'.

'Thinspiration'
64,000+
results on YouTube

3. Pro-ana and pro-mia websites

Many eating disorders sufferers frequent the 20 million 'pro-ana' (pro-anorexia) and pro-mia (pro-bulimia) websites.

Binge eaters, anorexics and bulimics use these sites, looking for tips and tricks on how to suppress their appetite, purging techniques, ideas on how to lose weight fast, or to compete with fellow sufferers to lose the most weight. Users of these sites often share pictures of themselves labelled with the date and their weight, priding themselves on any weight loss achieved and spurring themselves on to lose more in response to the often unkind comments left by others.

'I was a few pounds overweight and needed support. I found a great site where everyone gave each other weight-loss tips. I shared a photo of myself and got 47 comments mostly saying how FAT I was. It really motivated me. I lost 3 stone with the help of that site.'

Pupils who talk about blogging or participating in online communities related to weight and dieting should be a cause for concern as even if this is entered into innocently, it can often spiral out of control.

4. The eating disorder voice

Eating disorders sufferers often talk about their illness as if it were an entirely separate entity from themselves. They often speak of the 'ED Voice' inside their head which will spur them on to eat more, eat less, purge more or exercise harder, depending on the nature of their illness. The ED Voice can drive sufferers to extreme behaviours that they would never normally have considered.

> 'I found myself drinking toilet water. DIRTY toilet water. I'd read online that it could give you dysentery which would make you lose weight. I was so disgusted at myself – but the voice in my head that had urged me on so many times before just kept saying 'one more sip...''

Sufferers often talk about their eating disorder being a way of controlling their chaotic world. Eating, purging or choosing not to eat is the one thing they feel they can control. But in reality, once an eating disorder has taken hold, the sufferer tends to be entirely out of control, with the eating disorder claiming more and more control over their behaviour and actions.

5. Increasing isolation

Once in the grip of an eating disorder, sufferers tend to find themselves increasingly isolated from friends and family. They no longer feel able to relate to others, as thoughts of food take over every waking moment. Often they will also lose interest in activities which they once enjoyed with their friends, choosing instead to spend time alone eating, exercising or purging.

Anorexics and bulimics are increasingly reluctant to socialise, since they are often terrified to eat in front of other people, or worried about not knowing their calorie intake with unfamiliar foods. They may also worry about how they'll be able to purge themselves of calories consumed at an unfamiliar location.

Friends may distance themselves, feeling that they no longer understand this person they were once close to. Often they will be concerned about their friend but unsure how to help or relate to them.

The life of an eating disorder sufferer is often very lonely; they may have only their eating disorder for company much of the time. Or, far more dangerously, they may find a whole new circle of virtual friends in pro-eating disorder websites.

It doesn't seem strange

To a bystander, it might seem quite obvious that a young person with an eating disorder needs to alter their behaviour in order to improve their physical and emotional health. This is often not the perception of the sufferer themselves, who may not even acknowledge there is a problem, may go to great lengths to justify their behaviour, or may find the idea of coping without their eating-disordered behaviour impossible.

'I don't eat too little, you eat too much. You're greedy.'

'They told me if I didn't eat I'd die. I didn't really care. I didn't think I deserved to be alive.'

'How else can I make myself feel happy and safe like I can when I eat?'

'Throwing up is just my way of controlling my calorie intake. At least I'm enjoying my food.'

Young people are often unaware or unbothered by the potential long-term impact of their eating behaviour on their physical health.

Physical effects – anorexia

Aside from weight loss, or weight gain, eating disorders can have a host of physical effects, particularly if they continue over long periods of time.

These include:

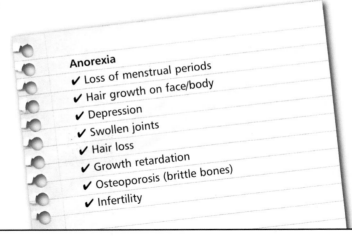

Anorexia
- ✔ Loss of menstrual periods
- ✔ Hair growth on face/body
- ✔ Depression
- ✔ Swollen joints
- ✔ Hair loss
- ✔ Growth retardation
- ✔ Osteoporosis (brittle bones)
- ✔ Infertility

Physical effects – bulimia and binge eating

Eating disorders also have the highest mortality rate of any mental health illness.

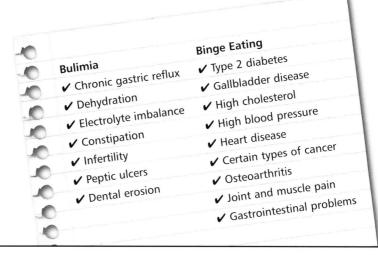

Bulimia
- ✔ Chronic gastric reflux
- ✔ Dehydration
- ✔ Electrolyte imbalance
- ✔ Constipation
- ✔ Infertility
- ✔ Peptic ulcers
- ✔ Dental erosion

Binge Eating
- ✔ Type 2 diabetes
- ✔ Gallbladder disease
- ✔ High cholesterol
- ✔ High blood pressure
- ✔ Heart disease
- ✔ Certain types of cancer
- ✔ Osteoarthritis
- ✔ Joint and muscle pain
- ✔ Gastrointestinal problems

Eating disorders at school

School can be a tough place to suffer from an eating disorder. Teasing or bullying can feel routine to sufferers, and there is an expectation to complete academic and physical activities every day.

'At my school you get teased if you're too thin and bullied if you're too fat.'

'I found it harder to understand and learn new things because my brain was starving.'

'I would look for any excuse to skip PE, I was so ashamed of my body.'

'At the beginning I did as much sport as possible to burn calories but soon I was too weak.'

Introduction
to Eating
Disorders

 Life with an
Eating Disorder

 Risk Factors
and Warning
Signs

 Encouraging
Pupils to Share
Concerns

 Talking it
Through

 Next Steps

 Practical
Support

 Keeping
on Track

Risk Factors
and
Warning Signs

Be on the lookout

Now that you understand a bit more about what eating disorders are, why people might suffer from them and the impact this can have on their lives, both short term and long term, you'll understand why it's important to do all we can to support those pupils who have issues with food, weight and eating.

This section of the book explains which pupils might be more likely to develop an eating disorder and are therefore worth keeping a close eye on. Then it identifies warning signs of each of the eating disorders.

As teachers or other members of school staff, you interact with pupils every day but are not as emotionally involved as friends and family. This places you in a very good position to spot eating disorder warning signs. Warning signs can often be apparent after holidays – whereas parents* may not notice a gradual change in behaviour or appearance, you may see a marked difference following a few weeks' break.

The term 'parents' is used throughout the book to cover parents/guardians/carers.

The importance of early detection

No one would consider leaving a suspected broken leg untreated; the same should be true of a suspected eating disorder.

Untreated broken leg	Untreated eating disorder
Short-term pain and suffering.	Untold psychological and sometimes physical pain for the sufferer. Each day you wait to act is another day of pain.
Pain causes distraction from academic work.	Academic work declines due to a preoccupation with food and brain starved of nutrients.
Pupil less likely to socialise due to pain and difficulty getting around.	Pupil socially isolates themselves, choosing not to go out with or even talk to close friends and family.
Injury worsens and may heal incorrectly. Treatment becomes more complicated and may involve an operation or long course of physiotherapy.	Eating disorder takes grip; later treatment may involve hospitalisation, medication and many months of therapy.
Pupil may never fully recover, being prone to further breaks and may be left with a limp.	Likelihood of long-term physical impact increases. Relapses are more likely and there is a reduced chance of a full recovery if treatment is delayed.

Detecting eating disorders early

It's clear from the broken leg analogy that early detection, treatment and support of eating disorders leads to significantly better outcomes for the sufferer. If we understand both the **risk factors** and **warning signs** we can be in a position to intervene as early as possible.

Risk factors
Some young people will be more at risk than others of developing an eating disorder in the first place so we should keep a closer eye on them for warning signs.

Warning signs
There are clear behavioural and physical warning signs which indicate a young person may be developing or suffering from an eating disorder. Learning some of these warning signs will mean you're well placed to spot potential eating disorders before they progress too far.

A wide range of risk factors

The next pages talk you through the most common risk factors and warning signs, but don't feel like you have to learn them all by heart. Use this as an awareness-raising exercise and come back to the book for a refresher whenever you feel alarm bells ringing.

None of the **risk factors** we'll go on to discuss mean that a young person *will* develop an eating disorder, but a pupil who has a combination of the different factors may be more *likely* to develop an eating disorder than their peers. So it's worth keeping a closer eye on them for warning signs.

There is a wide range of eating disorders **warning signs**; if you become aware of any pupil displaying several warning signs, it's worth investigating further. Even if it turns out that they don't have an eating disorder, the chances are they are in need of help and support.

Risk factors – personality

Personality traits that make a young person more likely to suffer from an eating disorder include:

- **Difficulty expressing feelings and emotions.** A young person who struggles to put into words what is bothering them may turn to food instead. (We all occasionally do this, reaching for the chocolate after a difficult day at work.) They may appear anxious, withdrawn, quiet or sensitive

- **A tendency to comply with others' demands.** Well-behaved students who abide by the rules are far more likely to get sucked into the world of eating disorders, where they often create a whole series of food rules for themselves

- **Very high expectations of achievement.** Pupils with a streak of perfectionism who think they've failed when they get a B are more prone to eating disorders. Their perfectionism can see them striving for a 'perfect' body whilst their determination gives them the skills and strength needed to diet to extremes

Risk factors – home life

A young person's home environment can have an impact on the likelihood of their developing an eating disorder. Particular risk factors include:

- **Emphasis on weight, appearance and dieting.** Growing up in a household where dieting is the norm and thinness is valued can encourage young people to look for ways to control their weight

- **An over-protective or over-controlling home environment.** Young people who feel they have no control over their own life and choices may turn to food as an aspect of their life over which they can exercise control

- **Poor parental relationships and arguments.** Food can be a refuge from many different types of problems. One such problem is difficult relationships at home

- **Neglect, or physical, sexual or emotional abuse.** It is quite common for sufferers of neglect, physical, sexual or emotional abuse to develop unhealthy coping mechanisms such as eating disorders, self-harm or reliance on drugs

Risk factors – extra-curricular activities

Some extracurricular activities can put pupils more at risk of developing an eating disorder if they encourage low weight, a trim physique or high fitness levels.

These include:

- Gymnastics
- Dancing
- Body building
- Boxing and wrestling
- Swimming
- Running
- Judo and martial arts
- Rowing or coxing
- Modelling

Of course, many young people engage in these activities healthily and safely. They shouldn't be discouraged from participating unless they're displaying eating disorder warning signs.

If you are involved in sports coaching be aware that your attitude to weight, physique, diet and fitness will have a strong influence on the young sportsmen and women you train.

Risk factors – weight loss

If an overweight pupil loses a few pounds it tends to result in positive feedback and compliments. This may motivate them to continue with their weight loss, sometimes beyond levels which are healthy.

It's not unheard of for very overweight pupils to become clinically anorexic within just a few months. These students can be particularly vulnerable if they have previously been teased or bullied about their weight.

Overweight pupils embarking on a weight-loss diet should do so with the support of their GP and parents to ensure that the weight is lost healthily. Keep an eye on any young person who loses a notable amount of weight, even if they are still overweight.

- **Up to half of young girls fear becoming fat and engage in dieting or binge eating**
- **One third of boys aged 8-12 have dieted to try to lose weight**

(All Parliamentary Party Group on Body Image Report, 2012)

Risk factors – peers

- **Fitting in**. Spending time with a group of friends who place a lot of emphasis on appearance and weight can increase the likelihood of a pupil developing an eating disorder – though many teachers may feel this applies to just about every teenager they've ever taught!

- **Bullying and teasing**. Pupils who have suffered bullying or teasing are more at risk of developing an eating disorder (and other mental health problems) than their peers, particularly, but not only, if the bullying is related to weight, shape or appearance.

It pays to be vigilant

Having covered the risk factors, let's now look at the **warning signs** of anorexia, bulimia and binge eating disorder.

Remember that whilst some pupils are more at risk than others of developing an eating disorder, nobody is exempt. If you see several of these warning signs in any of your pupils, it's worth following up.

> 'I just knew something was wrong. I should have said something sooner but it seemed so unlikely. She just wasn't the 'eating disorders type', if you know what I mean.'

Anorexia – warning signs

All eating disorders sufferers will tend to hide their behaviours and symptoms, so it can take an eagle eye to spot a problem. Anorexia warning signs include:

- **Weight loss** – the most obvious sign though often cleverly hidden
- **Restricted eating**, eg eating less or cutting out food types such as meat or dairy
- **Skipping meals** – pupils regularly skipping meals should be a cause for concern
- Scheduling activities during lunch so as to be '**too busy to eat**'
- **Strange behaviour** around food, eg ritualistic behaviours like cutting food into tiny pieces
- **Counting calories** – many anorexics know the calorie content of hundreds of foods
- Wearing **baggy clothes** to hide weight loss or prevent people seeing their 'fat' body

Anorexia – warning signs

- Wearing several **layers of clothing** to keep warm, even in summer

- Increasing **isolation**. Often an anorexic's only friend is their eating disorder

- **Believing they're fat** when they're not. Anorexics have a distorted body image

- **Avoiding PE or swimming** – they are ashamed of their bodies / hiding weight loss

- Alternatively spending **excessive amounts of time exercising** to lose weight

- Not eating enough to sustain them leads to **dizziness, lethargy and fainting**

- **Blue hands** – as fat stores deplete hands take on a bluish tinge due to feeling cold

- **Dull or lifeless hair** and **brittle nails** due to poor nutrition

Bulimia – warning signs

Bulimia is a very secretive disease. It's the most likely of the eating disorders to go undetected as sufferers will often remain at a roughly normal weight. Warning signs:

- Often **chewing gum/drinking water** to mask the smell of vomit
- **Visiting the toilets after meals** – can be a sign of vomiting or laxative abuse
- **Secretive behaviour** – bingeing and purging will often happen in secret
- **Weight fluctuation** – it goes up during binge periods and down during dieting periods
- Vomiting can lead to **swollen glands** and a **puffy face**
- **Callused knuckles** due to regularly inducing vomiting
- As a side-effect of repeated vomiting **sore throats/mouth ulcers**
- **Tooth decay** – acid in vomit erodes tooth enamel
- Consumed with thoughts of food they **can't focus on their school work**

Binge eating disorder – warning signs

Binge eating disorder often goes unspotted as many people assume that the sufferer is simply greedy. Of course, not all overweight people have binge eating disorder so here are some warning signs to look out for:

- **Weight increase** as a result of high calorie intake
- Feeling embarrassed/ashamed of eating when overweight, sufferers **tend to eat alone**
- **Eating very quickly** – sufferers eat rapidly and compulsively spurred on by their illness
- **Eating when not hungry** – may eat when bored, angry, upset, rarely due to hunger
- **Emotional eating** – using food as way of dealing with difficult situations
- Sufferers want to eat less but physically can't. They **feel out of control about their eating**
- **Seems moody or depressed** – follow up any significant changes in mood
- Consumed with thoughts of food they **can't focus on their school work**

Weight changes should trigger alarm bells

There are many warning signs and they do vary between eating disorders, so if you're ever concerned about a pupil, it will pay dividends to come back and consult these lists. However, the one warning sign that should have the alarm bells ringing above all others is a noticeable change in weight.

Whether a pupil has lost weight, gained weight or seems to have a fluctuating weight, take a moment to consider whether there is cause for concern.

- Is this student at higher risk of developing an eating disorder than others? (pages 34-42)
- Is the weight change accompanied by other warning signs? (see pages 44-49)

If you're worried that a student might have an eating disorder, the section of this book entitled 'Talking it Through' outlines what to do next.

Diet or eating disorder?

When diets feel like the norm, it's worth knowing the signs that a pupil is taking a diet too far:

1. The diet is highly restrictive
Any pupil who is restricting themselves to very little food is a cause for concern. Anorexics will routinely aim to eat less than half their recommended calorie intake each day.

2. No slips or trips
Most people will slip up on their diet occasionally, or allow themselves a treat. This tends not to be the case with eating disorders sufferers who are very strict in their approach.

3. Cutting out whole food groups
Eating disorders sufferers will often cut out whole food groups such as meat or dairy. Rather than simply looking for lower fat alternatives, they go a step further.

4. Always eats the same food
Eating disorders sufferers may find a meal or two that they consider 'safe'. They will often consume these same meals day in, day out, too scared to try something different.

Stats and figures

- 1.6 million people in the UK are living with an eating disorder
- Girls as young as 5 are worried about their size and the way they look

(All Party Parliamentary Party Group on Body Image Report, May 2012)

- 1 in 20 young women have eating habits which give cause for concern *(Mind)*
- 13-19 year-olds are most at risk of developing eating disorders *(Clinical Knowledge Summaries Service)*

- Almost a quarter of children aged 7-18 consider themselves overweight
- 40% of under-10s are worried about their weight
- 26% of 7-18 year-olds have skipped a meal to lose weight

(YouGov Poll, 2011)

Based on figures released by 35 NHS hospitals in England, between 2008 and 2011:

- More than 2,100 children under 16 were treated in hospital for eating disorders. Almost 600 of these were below the age of 13, including nearly 100 children aged between 5 and 7.

(The Telegraph, July 2011)

Introduction
to Eating
Disorders

 Life with an
Eating Disorder

 Risk Factors
and Warning
Signs

 Encouraging
Pupils to Share
Concerns

 Talking it
Through

 Next Steps

 Practical
Support

 Keeping
on Track

Encouraging
Pupils to Share
Concerns

A problem shared

As well as looking for risk factors and warning signs, another way to ensure we find out about eating disorders as early as possible is to create an environment where pupils feel confident about approaching a member of staff if they are concerned about themselves or a friend. This is important because it can mean that the school becomes aware of the problem earlier than it might otherwise be noted by even the most vigilant member of staff. This increases the chance of a positive outcome.

Unfortunately, research shows that pupils are very unlikely to voice their eating disorders concerns to a member of school staff. In this section we'll unpick the reasons for young people's reluctance to share their concerns and look at practical approaches you can take in your school to overcoming these barriers.

Why pupils don't confide

The six most common reasons pupils give for not confiding in school staff about eating disorders are summarised in these comments from teenagers:

1. Privacy — 'Our teachers don't have offices or anything so it's virtually impossible to speak to a teacher in private.'

2. Confusion — 'I'd probably have just built up the nerve to talk to a teacher and I'd be told, 'Sorry, you're not supposed to speak to me about this, you have to speak to X'.'

3. Trust — 'Teachers can't be trusted. They'd barge into the situation, mishandle it, and I'd lose the trust of my friend.'

4. Parents — 'They'd tell my friend's parents without even discussing it with my friend first and that would just make things worse.'

5. Knowledge — 'They wouldn't know what to do; they don't know anything about this kind of stuff.'

6. Anonymity — 'I'd want to be able to be anonymous – at least at first.'

Overcoming barriers

'Our teachers don't have offices or anything so it's virtually impossible to speak to a teacher in private.'

Teachers' suggestions for overcoming this barrier

- Set aside a time each week when you'll be available in your classroom at break and make pupils aware of this, especially pupils in your tutor group

- Set up a system where pupils can request an appointment with a teacher

- Create a schedule in which you speak privately for a few minutes with every member of your tutor group at least once each half term so they can raise any concerns

Overcoming barriers

'I'd probably have just built up the nerve to talk to a teacher and I'd be told, 'Sorry, you're not supposed to speak to me about this, you have to speak to X'.'

Teachers' suggestions for overcoming this barrier

*   The first step is for the school to have a clear policy and guidance on how a disclosure should be handled. This needs to be communicated to staff and pupils

*   Have a policy that states *any* member of staff can handle a disclosure. This way it is up to a pupil to decide who they feel comfortable talking to

*   If only certain members of staff are allowed to handle disclosures ensure that this is made clear to pupils and that those members of staff are readily available

Overcoming barriers

'Teachers can't be trusted. They'd barge into the situation, mishandle it, and I'd lose the trust of my friend.'

Teachers' suggestions for overcoming this barrier

- This problem is one of misconception. Set up clear guidelines about how eating disorders disclosures will be handled and share these with pupils

- Help younger pupils understand these guidelines by covering them in a PSHE or tutor session then having pupils design a poster explaining them

- In tutor periods, assembly, or PSHE, share an example of an anonymous pupil from the past and explain how the school supported and helped them to get better

- Explore themes of trust and friendship with pupils and work through examples which show that as a true friend you sometimes have to do something that might make your friend upset or angry in the short term, but is worthwhile if it helps them in the long term

Overcoming barriers

4. Parents

'They'd tell my friend's parents without even discussing it with my friend first and that would just make things worse.'

Teachers' suggestions for overcoming this barrier

- Pupils are particularly sensitive about parental involvement, but parents almost always *do* need to be involved. This should always be discussed with the pupil first

- Work with the pupil causing concern to decide exactly what their parents will be told and who'll tell them

- If a pupil has concerns about why a parent should not be told, hear them out. Their concerns will occasionally be genuine, eg an abuse situation may be worsened

- Offer to go with your pupil to their parents' home, or meet somewhere neutral if they think this will be preferable to meeting at school or talking on the phone

Overcoming barriers

5. Knowledge

'They wouldn't know what to do; they don't know anything about this kind of stuff.'

Teachers' suggestions for overcoming this barrier

- Ensure that all teachers have up-to-date training on eating disorders and make sure all pupils know this

- Teach pupils about eating disorders during PSHE or tutor time. This will show pupils that their teachers do understand these illnesses and take them seriously

- Be honest with pupils and explain that as a teacher, you don't always know the answer to everything but that you will always do your best to help them

Overcoming barriers

6. Anonymity

'I'd want to be able to be anonymous – at least at first.'

Teachers' suggestions for overcoming this barrier

- Share an email address that pupils can anonymously contact if they are concerned about themselves or a friend. Once you've gained their trust, they'll share their name

- Set up a simple post box system for pupils to share suggestions, complaints and concerns anonymously

- Make it clear to pupils that they will never be judged for anything they choose to share with you and they should not be afraid to voice their concerns

Action plan for overcoming barriers

It's likely that several of the barriers we've discussed are present in your school. Look back through the last few pages and consider what factors might stop a young person from sharing concerns about an eating disorder with a teacher in your school. For every barrier you identify, consider:

- Possible ideas for addressing this
- Who needs to be involved?
- Success criteria
- Next steps

You may find it helpful to work in conjunction with other staff, and pupils too. Brainstorming barriers with pupils in your tutor group will help you to overcome some of them.

It's worth knowing that, despite a real reluctance to confide, according to eating disorders charity 'Beat', children are still nine times more likely to talk to a teacher than a parent about their eating disorder.

Introduction to Eating Disorders

 Life with an Eating Disorder

 Risk Factors and Warning Signs

 Encouraging Pupils to Share Concerns

 Talking it Through

 Next Steps

 Practical Support

 Keeping on Track

Talking it Through

When should you say something?

As you become more familiar with the eating disorder risk factors and warning signs discussed earlier in this book; you'll find that from time to time a pupil begins to cause you concern. In this situation it can be very difficult to know when to say something.

The key thing to remember is that the more swiftly support is put in place, the better the long term prognosis. So if you're at all concerned about a pupil, then waiting isn't really appropriate; far better to go with your gut instinct and address the situation quickly.

If your fears are misplaced, the pupil will be able to put your mind at rest and explain the reasons for the behaviours you've been noticing*. And if you're right, you're likely to find that in the earlier stages of an eating disorder, the pupil will be scared and confused but far more likely to invite some form or help or support. Intervening when the illness is entrenched is likely to lead to a very different kind of conversation; once the eating disorder has a real grip you are likely to be met with resistance.

(See page 69 for what to do when pupils lie or deny.)

Detective work

Before you talk to a pupil, it can pay dividends to do some homework. Other staff and the pupil's peers may be able to give you some insight.

Talk to other staff
Have conversations with the person who oversees pastoral care in your school, the pupil's tutor and/or other member of staff who knows them well. They may have concerns of their own about the pupil, or may even be in conversation with them already. If you don't feel you are the best person to raise the matter with the student, you can ask one of these members of staff to talk to them instead.

Talk to the pupils' friends
Give the pupils' friends the opportunity to talk to you about any concerns they might have. If there is a problem these friends will be aware that something is amiss and will have been worrying about it and not knowing what to do. Usually, they will take the opportunity to share their concerns with you and you're likely to get a much better understanding of the problem this way.

Setting the scene

If you've decided that it's time to talk to a student about your concerns, rather than asking them to stay after class for an unspecified meeting, try to create more natural opportunities for them to talk to you privately.

If you can engineer a situation where the pupil feels they've instigated the conversation they will be more likely to open up. It doesn't need to be anything too clever: simply asking them to stay behind to discuss last night's homework is enough – then you should actually discuss the homework before asking casually, *'Are you okay? You seem awfully quiet'* or similar, which will hopefully instigate a deeper conversation.

If they don't open up to you, make sure you extend an open invitation for them to talk to you if they need help. *'If ever you need someone to talk to then remember you can find me in my room on Tuesday break times'*. This will give the pupil the chance to go away and think about whether they're ready to share their problems and it gives them a concrete time and place to return to when they're ready. Just make sure you are where you say you'll be.

Saying the right thing

The words that no pupil wants to hear are:

'I'm worried you might have an eating disorder.'

I'd advocate not using the phrase 'eating disorder' at all. It's a label that may not have occurred to the pupil and one that might terrify them. There is no need to pigeon-hole matters at this point. Your aim is to establish whether the pupil needs support.

Try to create an environment where you do most of the listening and the pupil does most of the talking. You can achieve this by asking open questions – ones that can't be met with one-word answers. (See next page.)

Take it slowly. You might not get to the nub of the problem during your first conversation, but at this point trust is the most important thing. Invite them to come and talk to you again tomorrow or next week. Once the pupil trusts you they will allow you enough insight to plan what you need to do next.

Asking the right questions

The right kinds of questions help people to open up about their problems, and prevent them feeling like they're being interviewed, eg:

- *'What are your biggest concerns at the moment?'*
- *'I've noticed you've not been yourself lately. How can I help?'*
- *'What would you like to talk about?'*
- *'Your friends are worried about you – do you know why that might be?'*
- *'How can I support you?'*
- *'What do you think we should do next?'*
- *'Why do you think that might be?'*
- *'Please can you explain a bit more about that?'*
- *'Is there a reason you feel that way?'*

Questions that don't have a simple answer will enable the pupil to explore their feelings and experiences and will make them realise that you're interested in their problems.

Don't talk, listen

Listening is the very best thing you can possibly do right now.

If a sufferer has come to you it's because they trust you and feel a need to share their secret with someone. Just let them talk. If necessary, ask occasional questions to encourage them to keep exploring their feelings and opening up to you. Just letting them pour out what they're thinking will make a huge difference and marks a significant first step in their recovery.

Up until now they may not have admitted even to themselves that they have a problem.

Ten tips for effective listening

1 Make enough time – don't embark on a conversation you won't have time to finish; instead agree a time and place to return to the conversation as soon as possible.

2 Remove physical barriers – sit next to or opposite the pupil; a desk between you can feel intimidating and make the student hold back.

3 Maintain eye contact – to the extent that it feels comfortable.

4 Minimise distractions – turn off your phone, computer etc. Focus solely on the pupil.

5 Keep an open mind – don't second guess the pupil. Make no assumptions, just listen.

6 Make 'listening noises' or actions – small responses show you're tuned in.

7 Ask exploratory questions – show you've understood and want to know more by asking a question that probes a little further.

8 Don't be scared of silence – allow the pupil time to think. If you just keep quiet they are likely to continue to explore their feelings.

9 The 80-20 rule – if the pupil is talking less than 80% of the time redress the balance.

10 Prove that you're listening and understand by occasionally paraphrasing.

Responding to denial

When confronted with concerns about their eating, it's relatively common for someone with an eating disorder to deny that there is a problem. If you find yourself in this situation, there are a few strategies you can try:

End the conversation but leave the door open – if you really don't think you're getting anywhere, draw the conversation to a close and make it clear that you're willing to listen when they're ready to talk. They may return after they've had a chance to think.

Undershoot – say, 'So you really don't think there's an issue at all and I've got it all wrong?' If the pupil acknowledges a difficulty, however small, gently explore this with them.

Explore the issue through a third person – ask, 'Why do you think your friends are concerned about you?' They may suggest, and then dismiss, reasons but this can at least provide a starting point.

Wait – sometimes silence can work wonders. If a student isn't opening up, just stay quiet for a while. This can encourage them to continue talking and exploring their feelings.

Stay calm

'I was so disgusted I just got up and left the room.
We never talked about it again.'

Even if you suspected a problem, it can be very upsetting to hear a young person talk about their eating disorder. They may disclose potentially shocking details about the depths of their unhappiness, or extreme measures they've been taking to control their weight. This may evoke feelings of unhappiness, horror, revulsion or despair, but however you feel inwardly, try to appear calm and accepting outwardly.

It's incredibly hard for a student to confide in someone about their eating disorder, and a negative reaction will shake their confidence and delay their recovery. Even if you are horrified by what you hear, **use your best acting skills** to disguise that and respond positive and calmly.

Positive response checklist

Right now, your pupil needs to feel that you are not judging them, that you are on their side and that you are trying to understand and support them.

- Make occasional eye contact
- Use open body language – show your palms; don't cross your arms or legs
- Nod and make affirmative noises to show you're listening
- Acknowledge that this must be difficult for the pupil
- Let the pupil know you're proud of them for taking this difficult step
- Don't take notes or openly check the time
- Plan with the pupil what happens next, or when you'll talk again

Try their shoes for size

The concept of an eating disorder can seem completely alien if you've never suffered from one. You may find yourself wondering why on earth someone would do these things to themselves, but don't explore those feelings with the pupil. Instead, listen hard to what they're saying; try to understand why they feel the need to use food as a coping mechanism and slowly start to understand what steps they might be ready to take in order to begin making some changes.

What they're thinking

 Positive experiences of confiding in a teacher

 Negative experiences of confiding in a teacher

'It meant a lot just to know someone cared. I was a bit worried about what would happen next but it was a relief to finally talk about it all.'

'Once I started talking about it, I couldn't stop. He just listened. Really listened.'

'I was worried that she'd think I was crazy but she seemed to really understand.'

'I could tell he thought I was disgusting. He couldn't bear to look at me.'

'It was so hard to be honest and tell someone what was going on, but she just dismissed it. She didn't get it at all. Didn't even try to.'

'She kept saying 'I'm listening' and 'I understand' but then she'd be picking her fingernails or looking at her watch like she didn't really care at all.'

A word on confidentiality

NEVER promise a pupil you will keep their concerns confidential.

It can be very tempting, especially if they preface a conversation with, *'I want to talk to you about something, but you can't tell anyone…'* Don't fall into this trap.

If a pupil is in need of support, you need to be able to share your concerns with other members of staff and the pupil's parents as appropriate. This thought may distress the pupil but it's best to be honest from the start. That way you are far less likely to jeopardise your relationship than by inevitably betraying their trust further down the line.

You can and should promise to involve the pupil in any further conversations you have about them. You can discuss **who** you need to talk to and **why**; **what** you will tell these people and **how**. You might choose to have the pupil present for some of these conversations.

Be prepared

Despite the fact that a sufferer has confided in you and may even have expressed a desire to get on top of their illness, that doesn't mean they'll readily accept help. Even if a pupil wants to recover, it's likely to be a long slow process.

Even if they want help they'll find it hard to accept

The eating disorder will control them, ensuring they resist any form of help for as long as they possibly can.

Don't be offended or upset if your offers of help are met with anger, indifference or insolence; it's the disease talking and however frustrated you are, keep calm. Anger never helps and will just drive a divide between you and the pupil who has put their trust in you.

Ending the meeting

When a student has confided in you about their eating disorder, whilst it will have been far from a formal meeting, it is important to confirm a few things to ensure that you both understand each other and that you are in agreement about how next to progress.

1. **Make clear that you're proud of them** – confiding in you took a great deal of courage. Acknowledge that and make it clear that they are no longer fighting this alone.
2. **Summarise what you've discussed** – ensure you've understood what the pupil's main concerns are and what they need help with. This does not need to be very detailed.
3. **Talk about aims for recovery** – acknowledge that there is no quick fix, but talk about the fact that you hope to work with them and other key people to help fix things.
4. **Agree action points** – agree the next steps. You need to make sure that these are simple and that the pupil understands the need for these actions.

Agreeing action points

The next steps will vary depending on how severe the problem is, what your school's policy is for handling eating disorders, how involved you will personally remain, who else needs to be involved and how ready the student is to seek help.

Possible action points might include:
- Arranging an appointment to see the head of pastoral care together
- Informing other members of staff
- Meeting with the pupil's parents
- Agreeing a time to meet again soon to discuss things further
- Meeting the pupil's form tutor to hand over
- Booking an appointment with the school counsellor
- Informing a trusted friend of the pupil and asking for their support

Be sensitive to the fact that the pupil may be unsure about divulging details of their problem to others. You may be the first person they have ever shared the information with. Try to strike a balance between being firm about the need to involve other people, and being sensitive to how difficult this may be.

Informing other members of staff

Once it becomes clear that a pupil has a problem surrounding food that will require help and support to overcome, it is important to involve relevant members of staff. This should be done with the agreement of the student and needs to be treated very sensitively.

So that the school can offer appropriate support, several members of staff will need to be aware of the situation. These may include the head teacher, the head of pastoral care and the pupil's form tutor. It is not necessary to announce the problem to all school staff. Despite best intentions this can make the student feel very uncomfortable as they are treated differently or watched.

Make sure that the pupil knows exactly **who** will be told, exactly **what** they will be told **when**, and **why** you feel it is important to inform them.

Next Steps

Where do you now stand?

You may or may not continue to be personally involved beyond this point. It is entirely appropriate to continue if you feel comfortable and the pupil would prefer it, but it is not essential.

Once the appropriate members of staff have been informed, depending on your school's policy, responsibility for the pupil is likely to lie with the head of pastoral care, headteacher or child protection officer. (A sample eating disorders policy can be downloaded from www.eatingdisordersadvice.co.uk/policy)

The rest of the book is mainly aimed at helping relevant members of staff support pupils with eating disorders and explains how to work with parents and external agencies and how to put strategies in place to support the pupil in school. Even if you are unlikely to be involved in these more advanced stages of support, reading on will give you a broader understanding of what will happen to the pupil once you hand the case over, and will give you some practical ideas you may wish to bear in mind during their recovery.

Forming a recovery team

In order for a pupil to recover from an eating disorder, they will need the support of a wide range of people who can be brought together to form a 'recovery team'. Such a team can ensure that a student feels consistently supported and is not receiving conflicting advice.

A trusted member of staff needs to work with the pupil to determine who will form the recovery team. It's important that the pupil feels in control of the process and that they trust everyone on the team. Possible team members include:

- One or two **close friends** who can offer insight as well as day-to day-support
- The **form tutor** who can look out for the pupil's best interests and negotiate with other staff as appropriate, eg if the pupil's homework load needs to be lightened
- **Parents**, who can offer continuity of care and support outside of school hours

Others, such as a **counsellor**, **educational psychologist**, **GP** or **psychiatrist**, may be brought on board once the pupil is working with them. The basic team should be informed and assembled as quickly as possible.

The role of the recovery team

The term 'recovery team' sounds formal – but it's not intended that way at all. The idea is simply to involve a group of people who are important to the pupil in supporting them to beat their eating disorder. The group's role is to offer support, guidance and practical help in overcoming day-to-day difficulties, eg lessons that make the pupil feel uncomfortable, or responding to inquisitive peers.

Recovering from an eating disorder is extremely hard work and things that might seem insignificant to others, such as entering the school cafeteria, or doing less well than usual on their school work, can feel insurmountable to the sufferer. With a team of people they can rely on for support, they are far more likely to succeed.

Exactly how the team functions should depend on the student's needs and wishes. Usually they lead the team with the help of a friend or chosen teacher. At first it can be helpful to meet as often as once a week but as the recovery progresses, meetings can become less frequent. Most pupils report that they prefer meetings that are brief, informal and focused on practicalities rather than on their eating disorder. The tone should always be positive.

Overcoming objections to working with parents

Parents should routinely be involved with their child's recovery from an eating disorder. They are in a great position to offer valuable support, particularly outside of school hours.

However, if a pupil chooses to confide in a teacher before a parent, it's not uncommon for them to object to their parents being informed. It's important to overcome this whilst remaining supportive to the pupil. Some suggested responses to common objections:

'I don't want to worry them.'

'I'm sure your parents are already worried. Once they know that you're trying to get better they'll be a lot less worried.'

'My parents won't understand.'

'You may be right, but I'm sure they'll want to learn to understand and to help you. I'll be with you to help explain things to them.'

'They'll get angry or upset.'

'They might do, but if they do, it will be because they're concerned about you. We can talk to them together.'

Inviting parents on board

Once a pupil has agreed to involve their parents, it's important to set up a meeting that strikes the right chord and can get the school-pupil-parent relationship off on the right foot. In this relationship, everyone should be seen as equal, with the pupil in the driving seat.

Talk to the pupil about where the meeting should be held, either at school, at their home or somewhere neutral. You should also discuss what will be said in the meeting and who will be leading it. The pupil may want to lead the meeting with your support, or may choose not to be present for the start of the meeting.

Understandably, parents can feel angry, confused or upset in these meetings. It's important to make clear that nobody is to blame and that the focus of this meeting is to offer support to the pupil and make plans for their recovery. Your aim is to share with parents the difficulties that their son or daughter has been facing and to invite them to be involved in the recovery process.

Inviting parents on board

make sure there is plenty of tea, it gives people something to divert their attention to at difficult moments

the pupil may wish to bring a friend for moral support

let the pupil choose which parts of the meeting they want to be present for

hear everyone out and discourage interruptions

you may need plenty of these!

a round table, or no table is less confrontational

Tips for meeting with parents

 Try to be objective when outlining the problem rather than injecting too much emotion. *'We think Joe may be suffering from bulimia. Bulimia is....'* is better than. *'Joe has had us so worried; he's constantly making himself sick and he seems so down.'*

 Don't analyse why the problem has arisen but rather focus on the practical steps that need to be taken to aid the pupil in their recovery. In most instances you should ask the parent or carer to take the child to their GP who may refer them on for further treatment.

 Keep the meeting informal, (though you should make and share notes afterwards) and be prepared to explore some difficult emotions. Ensure you have plenty of tea and plenty of tissues and enter the meeting with an open mind.

 Remember, the purpose of the meeting is to bring everyone together, to help the pupil inform their parents, and to decide clear next steps. These are often as simple as deciding a time to meet again and asking the pupil and parents to visit their GP.

 Make sure you share your contact details with the parents so they can get back in touch with any concerns or questions.

Parents – dealing with difficult scenarios

Whilst most parents are supportive, there are some relatively common negative reactions. Some parents go on the defensive, thinking you are accusing them of poor parenting and blaming them for their child's difficulties; others will think that you are over-reacting or getting involved in a matter that has nothing to do with you. How can you respond?

1. **Parents feel blamed**. Accept that the news may come as a horrible shock to parents. Calmly explain that no blame is intended. You think they are good parents, which is why you're seeking their support and help.

2. **Parents minimise the problem**. Explain exactly what is causing your concern and why you think there is an issue. Parents who react like this are sometimes unaware of the existence of eating disorders. You may need to help them learn about such disorders and their ramifications.

3. **Parents see problem as personal**. Occasionally a parent will feel that this type of concern is beyond the school's remit and should be dealt with solely at home. Explain how the school will be able to offer support and guidance and discuss with them, on a basic level, that as the child spends half their time in school, the school does need to be involved.

Talking to parents on the phone

It's always preferable to inform a parent of their child's eating disorder in a face-to-face meeting where you can read and respond to body language. However, It's not always possible and you may end up having to have the conversation on the phone. In which case:

- Ask the pupil which of their parents would be better to speak to
- Make a list of the points you want to cover beforehand
- Pre-arrange a good time to call so that both you and the parent have time to talk
- Always call from a landline whilst sitting at your desk. Focus only on the call
- Don't beat about the bush; the parent will want to know why you're calling
- Invite them to share their concerns; they are likely to be aware of a problem
- Make it clear that you're calling both to inform them, and to ask for their help and support
- Give them plenty of space to explore their concerns or ask questions
- Encourage them to meet you in person to discuss further

Peer support

It can be a good idea to include close friends of the pupil in the recovery team (as long as the pupil is happy with this) because:

- They will be very motivated to help their friend get better
- They can provide consistent support throughout the school day, eg by deflecting difficult questions, or explaining why the pupil hurriedly left a lesson
- They will be in a very good position to spot warning signs if things go wrong
- They will be able to act as a 'buffer' between their friend and inquisitive peers

If you do involve friends of the sufferer, ensure that you:

- Agree with the pupil exactly what their friends will be told
- Check that friends are happy to be involved and know that they can withdraw at any time
- Explain the pupil's problems carefully and answer any questions
- Do not put undue pressure on the friends – simply ask them to support
- Provide someone with whom friends can share their worries and concerns
- Have a clear agreement about what can and cannot be shared with other friends

External sources of support

In most instances, the pupil should be referred, with the support of their parents/carers to their GP. The GP will be in the best position to advise what specialist help and services are available locally and will be able to make a referral.

Help may be available through your local child and adolescent mental health services (CAMHS), a paediatrician, a dietician, specific mental health initiatives in your area or through private providers.

If a student is likely to be treated as an outpatient for some time, it is very helpful for the external agency to become involved in the school-based recovery team. This facilitates continuity of care and puts the school in the best possible position to offer support.

If a student is hospitalised or referred to a specialist unit for inpatient care, the school should retain regular contact with the care providers – and directly with the pupil if this is deemed appropriate.

Putting the pupil at the heart of the team

As we've discussed, a wide range of different people may be involved in the pupil's recovery. It's advisable to have these people work together as one team, with the aim of offering help and support to the pupil during recovery.

The most important job of this team is to empower the student in question to make steps towards their own recovery and enable them to embrace the daily challenges this will bring.

In order for a student to make a sustainable recovery, *they* have to drive the process. This may mean things move a little more slowly or that there is some discussion over recovery priorities, but there is no doubt that a fuller and longer lasting recovery will be made by a pupil who feels in control of the process.

Key pointers for helping the pupil feel in control

DON'T	✔ **DO**
• Talk about them as if they're not in the room (very easy to do!) • Dismiss their point of view even if you don't feel it's valid • Underestimate how difficult this is for them • Arrange meetings without checking the location/timing works for them	• Involve them in forming the recovery team • Ensure they are involved in discussions about their recovery • Discuss things using language that is accessible to them • Talk to them about how they'd like the room set up for meetings • Let them set the agenda (however informally) where possible. They will often want to discuss highly practical issues such as where they should eat their meals and with whom, whether they are allowed to participate in sport and who to talk to if they're having a difficult day • Offer continuous but unobtrusive support beyond meetings by making yourself available to them but never singling them out in front of their peers • Take time to praise them for their progress and involvement

Recovery team meeting logistics

There are no hard and fast rules about how often the recovery team, or parts of it, should meet in order to offer a pupil support. Let the pupil drive this where possible. It is useful to have at least one initial meeting with everyone involved in the pupil's recovery. This meeting should entirely revolve around the student, their needs, their recovery goals (see next page) and how the team can support these.

Encourage the pupil to discuss what they are currently finding difficult and what their goals are. The team's job is to determine how to help the student overcome these difficulties and support team-agreed goals.

The meeting should have an informal atmosphere in which everyone feels able to put forward their point of view. Make clear that the meeting is entirely confidential.

It can be useful to have fairly frequent follow-up meetings with smaller groups to ensure progress and tackle any difficulties as they arise. The only person who must attend every time is the pupil.

Recovery goals

One of the team's roles is to help the pupil work towards recovery goals. These should be determined by the pupil but agreed by the team as a whole. When goals are first set, it is very helpful to have present anyone formally involved in the recovery, eg a psychiatrist, educational psychologist or counsellor, as they'll be able to offer useful direction and focus.

The focus should be on **social and emotional goals** rather than food or weight goals. (These last two will be tackled by the student with their psychiatrist or counsellor.)

The goals can be quite simple and should each help address something the pupil is currently struggling with at school. They might include things such as:

• To come to school every day for a week
• To spend time with friends at break time
• To volunteer to read aloud in class

The goals should be achievable with the help of the team and everyone should give suggestions as to how they can support the student with each of their goals.

Academic expectations

The recovery team will need to address the academic expectations for the pupil and take into account the following:

1. **A brain struggling with an eating disorder is not best geared for learning.**
   The brain is a hungry organism which suffers abuse during an eating disorder. Starving the body denies the brain the energy needed for cognition, whilst bingeing produces sugar highs and lows that can make processing information difficult.

2. **Focusing on academic results can be unhelpful.**
   Teachers who are aware that a pupil is struggling with other difficulties may put a renewed emphasis on academic results, feeling that this is a positive focus. But students can easily end up obsessing over their work, just as they obsess over food, forfeiting sleep to achieve grades beyond their current capacity. If they try and fail, this can fuel their eating disorder.

'I wanted to be perfect. I tried so hard but I couldn't do the work like I used to. I stayed up all night and only got an A-. I punished myself the next day.'

Recovery is the focus. This may mean delaying exams or revising expectations.

When a pupil becomes an inpatient

If a pupil is considered seriously ill, they may need inpatient care, either in a paediatric or eating disorders unit. In this instance, the school should liaise with the healthcare providers about what level of contact is deemed helpful and appropriate. Some will encourage continuity with teachers, friends and academic work whilst others prefer to keep a student isolated during the early stages of recovery, gradually reintroducing them to their life as they get better.

With the agreement of the healthcare provider you could consider regularly providing work for the pupil, though there should be minimal pressure to complete it as the focus is on recovery. Sometimes it is considered appropriate for a teacher or teaching assistant to visit the pupil to tutor them too. Some units have schools on site.

You might also like to encourage the pupil's peers to keep in touch. This can help the pupil with the disorder realise that their friends care about and miss them. Friends might make a video, write emails or make a card. Again, there should be no onus on the student to respond. Seek guidance from the pupil's healthcare professionals about what contact would be useful.

Introduction
to Eating
Disorders

 Life with an
Eating Disorder

 Risk Factors
and Warning
Signs

 Encouraging
Pupils to Share
Concerns

 Talking it
Through

 Next Steps

 Practical
Support

 Keeping
on Track

Practical
Support

Guidelines for informing staff

It may become necessary to inform a wider range of school staff about a student's eating difficulties so they can support the recovery process.

Guidelines

- Decide with the pupil who needs to know (usually this will be their class teachers) and what information will be given

- Don't tell all staff unless necessary, as this can make the pupil feel uncomfortable

- Give staff clear directions about altering their academic expectations for the pupil (see pages 95 and 99)

- Provide staff with information about eating disorders and answer their questions

- Unless approached, staff should not discuss the pupil's problems with them

- Encourage staff to treat the pupil as normally as possible

- Make clear to whom staff should report concerns about the pupil

Responding to academic failure

Those who teach young people with eating disorders need guidelines on how to respond to their academic failure – or perceived failure – as this is a reality for pupils working towards recovery. Failing to achieve their usual grades can feel like the end of the world for someone whose eating disorder means they keenly define themselves in terms of success and failure.

When a student performs less well than usual, look for the positives. Try to find the success in this perceived failure. Emphasise what has been done well and elaborate on this in your marking or oral evaluation. However, never bump up a pupil's grades, or hide the truth about their performance, as learning to manage failure is an important lesson for those recovering from eating disorders. Sadly, this is a path fraught with failure both real and imagined.

Be aware also of the need to respond carefully to academic success. By emphasising academic achievements, you inadvertently put pressure on the young person to succeed. You may wish to consider limiting the amount of time the pupil should spend on any one piece of work to prevent them obsessing over trying to perfect it.

What NOT to say or do

During the recovery process, it can be very easy for eating-disordered thoughts to be triggered by someone saying or doing the wrong thing, even if they mean well. Almost any comment on appearance can be reinterpreted by the pupil as, *'You're fat'*.

Well-meaning comments such as: *'You're looking healthy'*; *'It's great to see some colour in your cheeks'*; *'You must feel better now you have more energy'* are all open to misinterpretation. **It's best to avoid any comment at all on a pupil's appearance**.

It's also important to be sensitive to tasks in class that may be difficult for the recovering pupil and to consider altering your scheme of work as necessary. Any tasks involving food, healthy eating and exercise, weighing or measuring the body in any way, or discussion of eating disorders are best avoided. If this is not possible, show the pupil all of the materials beforehand and allow them to opt out if they prefer.

Helpful things to say and do

Many teachers can feel so worried about saying or doing the wrong thing that they end up almost avoiding students they know to have eating disorders. What these pupils really need is to feel supported, included, valued and treated like 'normal' members of the class.

'My maths teacher said, 'How can I support you in my lessons?' and he took the time to listen to the answers and support me as I asked. That was fantastic.'

'I'd alienated my friends, so in group work there was no one to work with really. One teacher noticed and instead of letting us pick our groups he did it randomly which was better.'

'She just treated me normally whilst everyone else treated me with kid gloves. She even gave me a detention. I was kind of proud. Normal kids get detention...'

'If something tough was coming up, my psychology teacher scratched her ear to warn me. If I wasn't feeling up to it I left for a few minutes and no one said a word.'

'It only got a B, but my teacher read it out and praised it. Then I was proud of my B!'

Support for staff and peers

The ramifications of a pupil struggling with an eating disorder can reverberate throughout the staff and student body. It can make an impression on people you might not expect to be affected. Whilst it would be inappropriate to share details of specific cases with the entire school, it is important to ensure that everyone knows where to turn for eating disorders support if they need it.

> 'My friend's big sister was anorexic. I was scared she'd die. I didn't know who to talk to.'

Put up posters outlining where pupils can access support – either within the school or via external helplines or website. You may also want to cover the topic in PSHE or tutor time.

Remember, there may be staff who have themselves struggled with eating disorders. Seeing a pupil struggle in the same way may stir up difficult memories and emotions for them. Put up helpline numbers in the staff room and be vigilant for eating disorder warning signs in staff as well as students.

> 'It brought all my own battles back. Everyone said he looked really ill but I found myself thinking, 'I could be that thin again,' and soon I was well on the way.'

Talking to pupils

When a pupil has an eating disorder, their peers will know that there's a problem. Some will be concerned and want to know how to help; some will be scared and have a lot of questions; others may tease the pupil for being different.

For these reasons it's important to educate the sufferer's peer group about eating disorders and ensure there is a forum for them to ask questions and access support. Of course, the sufferer will not want their problems broadcast and this is a difficult balancing act.

Many schools find covering eating disorders during tutor time, in the absence of the sufferer, a good compromise. Make sure the pupil knows what will be covered with their peers and ask them about any particular concerns, eg weight-related teasing, so that these can be woven in to the discussion.

Alternatively, if a student feels confident enough to address their peers themselves (with a teacher's support) this can work well. Make sure they don't feel under pressure and can opt out of talking about anything that makes them feel uncomfortable.

Sharing with peers

> As I talked I remembered, 'These people are all my friends' – they were so supportive.'

If a pupil would like the opportunity to discuss their difficulties with their peers, only encourage it if it is agreed by any specialists involved with their care. There are several things you can do to support:

1. **Discuss what they'll say and to whom**. Run through with them what they will cover. Ensure they're comfortable with it and that you are too. Agree who'll be present – which students and would they like anyone else there?

2. **Talk about how it will work**. Agree how it will work, eg should you introduce the topic? Are they happy to have questions throughout, at the end, or not at all?

3. **Check for 'no go' areas**. Double check whether there are any areas they're really not happy to discuss. This will enable you to help steer the conversation.

4. **Use common sense**. If things feel uncomfortable, stop; if things go off-plan but everyone seems happy, carry on.

Five practical support strategies

These support strategies have all been suggested by pupils struggling with eating disorders and can be implemented in any school. They are explained over the next few pages.

1 Peer support.

2 Free pass.

3 Bolt hole.

4 Trusted adult.

5 Zero tolerance of bullying.

Day-to-day peer support

'The most useful thing of all was a friend. Feeling like there was someone on my side, someone who understood and could explain why I'd fled crying, really helped.'

Close friends of a pupil struggling with an eating disorder will usually be keen to be involved in supporting in any way they can and this can be a huge help, both to the pupil in question and to the school. Friends naturally take on a supportive role and by formalising this a little and becoming involved as a school you can make it even more beneficial to the pupil:

- Work with the sufferer and their friends to identify difficult situations that might arise and how the friends might support in these instances, eg in response to probing questions from a friend or if a lesson becomes unmanageable

- Teach the friends about eating disorders more generally and make them aware of relapse warning signs and how to raise the alarm

- Ensure the sufferer's friends are fully supported. They are going through a difficult time too and will need opportunities to discuss their feelings in confidence

Free pass

> 'Knowing I could get up and leave if I needed to made it easier to stay in the lesson.'

Pupils recovering from an eating disorder can suddenly find things difficult to cope with. This could be due to something in a lesson triggering difficult feelings, or down to something internal that they're struggling with. Either way, the prospect of making it through double maths whilst your whole world is caving in on you is a tough one.

Allowing pupils to absent themselves from lessons, with no questions asked can help considerably. Simply being able to walk away from a situation which has become too difficult to cope with can help the pupil to calm down and prevent the situation from escalating.

The pupil's teachers all need to be informed and fully supportive if this is to work, and the pupil or their friends need to be prepared to answer questions from peers. Generally speaking, pupils use their 'free pass' frequently to start with but quickly find themselves better able to manage in class.

Providing a bolt hole

'My body learnt that it was my 'safe place'. If I thought I was going to have a panic attack I went there, put my music on, breathed deeply and soon everything was okay again.'

As well as being able to leave lessons, it is useful for pupils to know there is somewhere safe and quiet they can go to calm down if things feel too much. It is not always easy to find such a safe haven in a school but suggestions from teachers include:

- The staffroom
- A teacher's office
- A 'chiller' or internal exclusion room (but not if it has negative connotations)

- A common room
- The sick bay/ medical room
- The library

It needs to be somewhere the pupil can easily access and where they are allowed any time they need to calm down, get away from a situation or compose themselves. They should not be expected to talk to anyone, unless they want to, and should be free to carry on with an activity that they find calming, such as listening to music, reading or drawing.

Regular access to a trusted adult

'I came to really value her support. Just knowing I would start my day with five minutes to discuss my concerns about the day ahead was brilliant.'

Pupils often highly value the support of a trusted adult in school. This may be a form tutor, a counsellor, a school nurse or another adult indicated by the pupil. It can be difficult in a school environment to find time to talk privately, so scheduling regular times for the pupil and their trusted adult to sit down together can often work very well. This might be as often as once a day or as little as once a week and may take five minutes or half an hour. It's all down to what is helpful for the pupil and practical for the member of staff.

- The pupil should direct the conversation
- They may find it comforting to talk about seemingly unrelated matters
- Explore any concerns the pupil may have, even if they seem trivial
- If the pupil doesn't turn up, don't reprimand them, even if time is wasted. However, if the adult can't attend they *must* inform the pupil

Zero tolerance of bullying

'I was told, 'ignore them, they're just teasing' but I couldn't ignore them. I was so sensitive at that time that the slightest thing could trigger a bad food day.'

It's very common for pupils with eating disorders to be bullied or teased for being too thin, too fat, or just simply for being different. And not just by pupils, by staff too.

'My maths teacher joked about me being fat. I was skin and bones but took him seriously.'

Your school should adopt a zero tolerance approach to food, weight and shape-related teasing and bullying, especially when you have a recovering pupil in your midst.

- Treat all comments, jokes and rumours about food, shape and weight seriously
- Educate pupils about eating disorders to remove some of the stigma
- Make it easy for pupils to share their anxieties about being teased or bullied
- Remove the taboo from the staffroom. Let staff learn and talk about eating disorders
- Have a clear and consistent policy on bullying – and implement it

Ideas for mealtimes

Mealtimes can be particularly difficult, both at home and at school, for pupils recovering from an eating disorder. They need to feel supported without feeling pressured or spied on. Some helpful ideas include:

- Allowing them to eat at a different time to their peers
- Not questioning unusual combinations of food if that's what they want
- Offering alternative places for them to eat if a dining hall is too difficult
- Providing pre-agreed special meals if practical/ possible
- Letting them serve their own food if possible
- Not passing comment on how much/ little they have eaten
- If food diaries need to be kept, encouraging them to do this themselves
- Ensuring they never feel 'watched' whilst eating
- Making sure that eating disorder concerns are never discussed during a meal
- Offering the support of a friend or trusted adult to eat with them
- Trying to ensure they are busy and not alone following meals

One step forward...

However well a school supports a pupil with an eating disorder, it's important to remember that recovery is a long and difficult process and that it can feel like one step forward and two steps back.

Relapses or set-backs are not a reflection on how well the pupil is being supported, nor how hard they are trying. They are simply a fact of recovery. The pupil should be supported positively throughout and should NEVER be made to feel that they have failed or have let anyone down.

Keeping
on Track

Reintegration after absence

If a pupil is removed from school for a period of time due to an eating disorder, there are several things the school can do to ensure a successful return to school.

1. **Prepare staff.** Staff will be aware of the student's absence; they will need to know the reason for the absence and be given advice on how to support the student on their return.

2. **Prepare peers.** Other pupils will have questions about their friend and will want to know how to support them. Allow plenty of time to explore these issues prior to the pupil's return.

3. **Make contact with the pupil prior to their return.** It can be overwhelming to be suddenly plunged back into school life. Some contact from selected teachers and friends prior to a pupil's return can ease the transition.

4. **Work out where the academic gaps are.** Even if you've been providing work for the student during their absence, they're likely to have fallen behind. This should not be considered or presented as a problem, but teachers do need to be up to speed so they can revise their expectations.

Reintegration after absence

5. **Work with the external agency and parents.** Ensure that a relationship is established both with the agency that has been working with the pupil and with the parents. Work together with the pupil to create a plan for their return to school.

6. **Consider a phased return.** Allow the pupil to attend for just a few lessons a week at first and gradually build up to full days and full weeks.

7. **Acknowledge that the pupil has been away.** Whilst the absence shouldn't be dwelt upon, it shouldn't be ignored either. Don't publicly welcome a pupil back in assembly or similar, but ensure that close friends or their tutor group acknowledge their return.

8. **Implement the other ideas in this book.** There are lots of ideas about working with pupils in recovery in this book. These apply equally whether a pupil has remained in school or whether they're returning after a period of absence.

Monitoring progress

The school is in a good position to monitor the progress of pupils who are recovering from an eating disorder. Make progress monitoring unobtrusive and use it mainly for reassurance that things are headed in the right direction. You may choose not to share any form of monitoring with the pupil but where you do, make sure it is non-judgmental and matter of fact rather than a cause for celebration or a stick to beat them with.

Close monitoring is not vital but it can offer reassurance to all parties. Some schools choose to monitor:

✓ Attendance

✓ Participation in lessons and other activities

✓ Behaviour at mealtimes

✓ Frequency of reliance on a free pass or 'bolt hole'

✓ Academic performance

However, the school should not closely monitor food intake, weight or exercise, unless under the advice or guidance of an external agency such as the pupil's mental health worker.

Regular meetings

A recovering pupil should never feel alone or unsupported. Regularly meeting with the student and one or more of the following can be helpful:

- Their close friends
- Form tutor or other trusted adult at school
- Parents
- Mental health worker or similar

These meetings should be driven by the pupil and used to ascertain any problems or difficulties they are facing. Everyone involved should be looking for practical ways to support the student. (See pages 81-95 for guidance on forming and running recovery teams.)

What could go wrong?

Recovering from an eating disorder can be a complicated, difficult and often lengthy process. As we have seen, it is quite common to suffer setbacks. In particular pupils are prone to:

- **Relapse**
  A pupil who had been recovering well starts to display eating disordered behaviour again
- **A different eating disorder**
  Some people develop *different* eating disorder behaviours as they recover, eg an anorexic may begin to binge, a binge eater may begin to purge, etc.
- **Alternative unhealthy coping mechanisms**
  Without food to turn to, some people recovering from an eating disorder will turn to substance or alcohol abuse, risky sexual activities or other unhealthy coping mechanisms

You can help support a pupil through any of these eventualities as long as you are aware of them. So provide plenty of opportunities for the pupil to share their concerns with a trusted adult, and ensure that their friends remain vigilant.

How to handle a rough patch

If it looks like things are taking a turn for the worse, address matters head-on as quickly as possible, whilst remaining sensitive and supportive.

The pupil must not be made to feel that they've failed.
This is simply a setback and nothing more. Think of it as a detour rather than the end of the line.

Explore what has triggered the current difficulties.
It may be that a particular incident has caused this setback, perhaps something someone has said or done. The pupil needs to feel able to share this in confidence so similar situations can be avoided moving forward.

Offer more support if necessary.
It may be necessary to increase the amount of support you offer to the pupil for a while. Discuss this option and let them guide you.

Don't feel you have to go it alone.
If you feel it's appropriate, bring in the support of external agencies such as CAMHS, even if you had previously felt this was no longer necessary.

The importance of relapses

Whilst any form of relapse or difficulty during recovery can feel very depressing for everyone involved, it's important for the pupil to learn to work through these difficult periods. Right now they have a supportive team around them but this may not always be the case.

Work with the pupil to learn to identify the early signs that things aren't going quite to plan, and discuss with them how to make positive changes at this early stage before the eating disorder takes a firm grip again. Learning to self-monitor will stand them in good stead for times ahead when they may be living away from home, at university for example, without their old support network.

After a difficult patch it is not uncommon for a sufferer to approach their recovery with renewed vigour and determination.

What does success look like?

The number one priority is a healthy, happy pupil. It is unrealistic to expect that the pupil will never again suffer any difficulties with food. A big part of success is about the pupil **becoming sufficiently self-aware** to spot potential problems in their eating behaviour in time to prevent a major relapse in the future.

Successfully beating an eating disorder may involve making compromises such as:

- Deferring exams
- Performing less than perfectly in exams
- Withdrawing from high level competitions in a favourite sport or activity

These compromises may be seen as failures by the pupil, but they're not. If they are happy and choosing to eat healthily each day, then they are succeeding and should be proud.

Success stories – sufferers' points of view

'It was the hardest thing I ever had to do, but I did it. I haven't made myself sick for three years now. I have a steady job and a steady boyfriend; life is good!'

'A turning point was when I accepted that I wasn't just fat and greedy but that I had a proper problem and needed proper help. I don't binge anymore and if I feel the urge I know to try and work out what the problem is rather than just start eating. I'm getting closer to a healthy weight and I've actually started enjoying going out with my friends.'

'It's only now that I realise I could have actually died. I could literally have starved myself to death. At the time I probably wouldn't have cared but now I'm happy to be alive every day.'

'For me, success is no longer about having a string of A*s and the perfect body; it's about being alive, doing my best and learning to love myself. I'm not so bad...'

Success stories – staff members' points of view

'There were a lot of ups and even more downs, but we got there in the end. It was a real team effort involving friends, parents and staff at school. He's finished school now but he comes back to say hi, and let us know that he's doing okay. I think we became quite special to him, as he did to us.'

'I felt completely out of my depth when she first confided in me, but I'm so glad she trusted me to help. She'll soon be sitting her GCSEs, a year later than planned. Her predicted grades are good – but more importantly, she seems genuinely happy.'

'I had no idea how hard it would be to beat an eating disorder. She fought so hard and we were like her little army, behind her every step of the way. Life is beginning to return to normal for her now which is just wonderful to see.'

Websites, helplines, books

www.b-eat.co.uk *Beat* provides helplines, online support and a network of UK-wide self-help groups to assist adults and young people in the UK to beat their eating disorders. Their helplines are for anyone who needs support and information about eating disorders:

Adult Helpline (for parents or teachers) 0845 634 1414
Youth Helpline (for pupils) 0845 634 7650

www.eatingdisordersadvice.co.uk *Eating Disorders Advice* provides guidance and support for teachers and loved ones of eating disorders sufferers.

www.youngmindsinschools.org.uk *Young Minds in Schools* are committed to supporting the emotional wellbeing of all pupils. This website has lots of resources and advice for teachers on a range of mental health issues.

Skills-based Learning for Caring for a Loved One with an Eating Disorder: The New Maudsley Method
by Janet Treasure, Anna Crane and Gráinne Smith, Routledge, 2007.
This book provides a structure for talking to and supporting sufferers. Particularly useful for parents, it is a good read for teachers too.

Acknowledgements

A huge thank you to the students and staff who have taken part in my research, and to my PhD supervisors Ulrike Schmidt and Janet Treasure who have been both inspiring and patient. Thank you also to my special teachers: Jane Bunclark, Alison Callow, Gill Fowles, Jane Moore, Kate Pouncey and Geraldine Rowland – I hope you find this book useful. Thanks finally to my friends and family, especially Tor Bryant, Izzie Jamal, and my husband Tom Hesmondhalgh. I wouldn't be here without you.

This book is based on work supported by the National Institute for Health Research (NIHR) under its Programme Grants for Applied Research Scheme (RP-PG-0606-1043).The views expressed herein are those of the author and not necessarily those of the NHS, NIHR or the Department of Health.

About the author

Pooky Knightsmith

Pooky Knightsmith is a specialist in working with school staff to prevent and manage eating disorders. She is currently researching a PhD on this topic at the Institute of Psychiatry. During the course of this research Pooky has worked directly with over 800 teachers and 500 pupils from a wide range of school settings.

Since graduating from Oxford, where she studied experimental psychology, Pooky has been working in the education sector, first with Creative Education Ltd as Director of Training and latterly with the Times Educational Supplement as Social Media Manager, engaging with a network of over 2 million educators.

Pooky is a seasoned school governor, having worked hands-on with three schools with a particular involvement in child protection issues. She has recently been invited to become a trustee for Beat – the world's leading eating disorders charity – to enhance their work in the education sector.

You can find further support and advice on Pooky's blog: **www.eatingdisordersadvice.co.uk** which is regularly updated with eating disorders advice for parents and teachers.

Pocketbooks – available in both paperback and digital formats

Teachers' Titles:

Accelerated Learning
Anger & Conflict Management
Asperger Syndrome
Assessment & Learning
Behaviour Management
Boys, Girls & Learning
Challenging Behaviours
Coaching & Reflecting
Creative Teaching
Differentiation
Drama for Learning
Dyslexia
Dyspraxia/DCD
EAL
Eating Disorders
Effective Classroom Communication
Emotional Literacy
Form Tutor's
Fundraising for Schools
Gifted & Talented
Handwriting
Head of Department's
Inclusion
Jobs & Interviews
Learning & the Brain
Learning to Learn
Lesson Observation
Managing Workload
Outstanding Lessons
P4C
Primary Headteacher's
Primary Teacher's
Promoting Your School
Pupil Mentoring
Restorative Justice
Secondary Teacher's
Stop Bullying
Teaching Assistant's
Teaching Thinking

Selected Management Titles:

Appraisals
Assertiveness
Coaching
Developing People
Emotional Intelligence
Energy & Well-being
Icebreakers
Impact & Presence
Influencing
Interviewer's
Leadership
Managing Change
Meetings
Mentoring
Motivation
NLP
Openers & Closers
People Manager's
Performance Management
Personal Success
Positive Mental Attitude
Presentations
Problem Behaviour
Resolving Conflict
Succeeding at Interviews
Stress
Storytelling
Teambuilding Activities
Teamworking
Thinker's
Time Management
Trainer's
Vocal Skills
Workplace Politics

Order Form

Your details

Name _____

Position _____

School _____

Address _____

_____

_____

Telephone _____

Fax _____

E-mail _____

VAT No. (EC only) _____

Your Order Ref _____

Please send me:

		No. copies
Eating Disorders	Pocketbook	☐
_____	Pocketbook	☐
_____	Pocketbook	☐
_____	Pocketbook	☐

Order by Post

Teachers' Pocketbooks
Laurel House, Station Approach
Alresford, Hants. SO24 9JH UK

Order by Phone, Fax or Internet
Telephone: +44 (0)1962 735573
Facsimile: +44 (0)1962 733637
Email: sales@teacherspocketbooks.co.uk
Web: www.teacherspocketbooks.co.uk

Customers in USA should contact:
2427 Bond Street, University Park, IL 60466
Tel: 866 620 6944   Facsimile: 708 534 7803
Email: mp.orders@ware-pak.com
Web: www.Teacherspocketbooks.com